Specification and Informational Issues in Credit Scoring

Nicholas M. Kiefer

nickkiefer@aol.com

and

C. Erik Larson

OCC Economics Working Paper 2004-5

Abstract:

Lenders use rating and scoring models to rank credit applicants on their expected performance. The models and approaches are numerous. We explore the possibility that estimates generated by models developed with data drawn solely from extended loans are less valuable than they should be because of selectivity bias. We investigate the value of "reject inference" – methods that use a rejected applicant's characteristics, rather than loan performance data, in scoring model development. In the course of making this investigation, we also discuss the advantages of using parametric as well as nonparametric modeling. These issues are discussed and illustrated in the context of a simple stylized model.

Nicholas M. Kiefer is a Professor in the Departments of Economics and Statistical Sciences, Cornell University, Uris Hall, Ithaca, NY 14853. C. Erik Larsen is a Senior Financial Economist at the Office of the Comptroller of the Currency's Risk Analysis Division, Washington, DC 20219.

1

Specification and Informational Issues in Credit Scoring

Nicholas M. Kiefer and C. Erik Larson

I. Introduction

Credit scoring models rate credit applications on the basis of current application and past performance data. In a typical application, credit performance measures and borrower characteristics are calculated as functions of the data for a sample of borrowers. These measures are then used to develop statistical scoring models, the output of which, scores, are forecasts of credit performance for borrowers with similar characteristics. For example, a model might generate a predicted performance measure as a function of the applicant's use, in percent, of existing credit lines. A lender will typically use this performance predictor as part of a decision on whether or not to extend credit in response to the application. A simple decision rule would be to accept the application only if the estimated performance measure (say, the probability of delinquency or default) is less than a critical value α. The appropriate performance metric may vary across applications. A natural metric in the stylized models we will discuss is default probability; although we found it useful to reference "default probability" throughout the paper, the discussion holds for essentially any performance measure. A practical, though more complicated approach, is to estimate a loan's profitability. We note that in retail banking practice, it is more common than not to report performance forecasts (scores) that increase in value as the probability of default decreases. In contrast, corporate and other business rating and scoring models are usually report scores and grades that increase with the probability of default. In the balance of this paper, and particularly in the examples, we make use of the latter convention.

Discussions of the credit scoring problem, including various approaches used in practice and treatment for different applications (mortgage lending, credit card lending, small commercial lending, etc.) are given by Thomas, Edelman and Crook (2002), Hand (1997), Thomas, Crook, and Edelman (1996) (a collection of relevant articles) and others. A recent review of the credit scoring problem including an insightful discussion of evaluating scoring mechanisms (scoring the score) is given by Hand (2001). Early treatments of the scoring problem are Bierman and Hausman (1970), and Dirickx and Wakeman (1976); this work has been followed up by Srinivasan and Kim (1987) and others.

A critical issue in credit modeling is the relevance of the data on the experience of loans extended to the potential experience of loans declined. Can the relation between default and characteristics in the sample of loans made be realistically extended to predicting the default probabilities for loans not made? This problem is known as a "selectivity" problem. A number of methods based on "reject sampling" have been proposed to try to use data from rejected loan applications together with the experience of existing loans.

A related issue is the relevance of the experience with loans presently or previously outstanding to current and future potential loans. Demographic changes (an aging population) or a different stage in the business cycle could diminish the relevance of such experience.

The procedure we examine is essentially sequential, though the full implications of the sequential updating process are not explored here. Loan applications are accepted according to some rule, possibly stochastic. The experience of these loans is recorded and used to estimate, or sharpen, existing estimates of default probabilities. Of course, repayment and default information is available only on loans that were extended. However, parametric data is available on rejected loans, and we explore the potential for bias in using the data only on accepted loans. We also address the possibility of using reject sampling schemes to improve scoring models or default risk estimates. Our simple framework abstracts key concepts at issue from some difficult practical problems (such as what exactly default is; how to account for loans applied for, accepted by the bank, and then declined by the applicant; and how default probabilities change over the duration of a loan). Finally, our focus on default as the outcome of interest is a useful abstraction: in practice it may be appropriate to study the expected profit performance of a given loan application. This involves the default probability, but adds other considerations.

Throughout we emphasize a key conceptual distinction between two closely related questions: Should the bank continue to make loans to applicants with marginally acceptable characteristics? Should the bank extend loans to applicants whose characteristics under current rules are marginally acceptable? There is data on the former question, as default probabilities can be directly measured from experience with loan performances. Because the latter question cannot be answered using this conventional data, we must turn to parametric assumptions or other methods of extrapolating from the given sample. The only reliable way to answer the second question is to use these parametric assumptions or collect additional information. We suggest carrying out experiments with the scoring rule.

II. A Stylized Model

A simple model allows concentration on key conceptual issues, though necessarily suppressing many practical questions. Suppose the profit from serving an account over a fixed period is π, the probability of default is p, and the loss given default is λ (defined here as a positive number). Then the expected profit from this account over the period (we will return to the question of the period) is $\pi(1-p)-\lambda p$. In this case, loans are profitable only if $p <= \pi/(\pi+\lambda)$. As a practical matter, banks should rank applicants according to the estimated value of p and extend loans to those applicants with the smallest default probabilities (as funds are available) up to the critical value $p* = \pi/(\pi+\lambda)$. Of course, there is a lot missing in this calculation, including the important question of estimation error in p and how that might vary across applicants.

A minor variation on this calculation can get around the awkward question of the definition of the period. Let us reinterpret profit as a flow, $\pi*$. Assume the discount rate is r. Let T, a random variable, be the time of default and suppose for simplicity that T is distributed exponentially with parameter a, $f(t) = ae^{-at}$. Then expected profit is given by

$$E(\text{profit}|T) = \int_0^T \pi*e^{-rt}dt - \lambda e^{-rT}$$

$$= \pi^*/r - (\pi^*/r + \lambda)e^{-rT}$$

and unconditionally

$$E(\text{profit}) \qquad = \pi^*/r - a(\pi^*/r+\lambda)/(r+a).$$

Again, we get a cutoff rule, order the applicants in terms of a and extend loans to those with the smallest values of a, up to the critical value. For a fixed period, there is a monotone map between a and p, the default probability in the previous model.

The point of this exercise is not to exhibit a realistic model, but to illustrate that the lesson from the simple model is fairly robust. Namely, the optimal lending policy will involve ranking applicants according to a performance measure and lending funds as available up to a cutoff point. Note that, as a practical matter, essentially all of the "fixed" parameters in the simple model will vary across applicants and possibly over time according to macroeconomic and local economic conditions.

III. Information and Identification

Suppose the application data consists of X. At present, X can be rather abstract, perhaps a collection of numbers indicating financial history, discrete or continuous variables, etc. On the basis of X, a decision is made whether to approve a loan application. Let Y be the variable indicating loan approval (Y=1) or decline (Y = 0).

Suppose the population relationship between default D' (=1 for default, 0 for no default) and data X is P(D'|X). The chain determining events is

$$X \rightarrow (Y,X) \rightarrow (D'^*Y , Y,X) = (D,Y,X)$$

where the final state consists of D' if it is observed, that is if $Y = 1$, and no information on D' if $Y = 0$. Here X determines Y and X is simply carried along as a determinant of D. The final state D is determined by Y and X.

The key observation here is that the intermediate state, (Y,X) contains no information not already contained in X. Y is determined as a (possibly random) function of X. For example, X might be the predictor variables in a default risk model and Y might be chosen to equal 1 (accept the application) if the predicted default probability is less than α. In this case, Y is a deterministic function of X. Alternatively, Y could be completely random, determined, for example, by a coin flip. In the language of the statistical literature on missing data, the mechanism determining Y and hence D is missing at random (MAR, Little and Rubin, 2002). The deterministic case, possibly relevant here, in which Y is determined by some function of X, is a special case of the MAR mechanism.

Since Y contains no information not contained in X, inference on $P(D'|X)$ does not depend on Y. Of course, this inference can only be made for X configurations actually observed. Which values are observed depends on X (and possibly a random mechanism), so there is no bias associated with estimating those probabilities that are identified. To illustrate, suppose X is binary and the deterministic selection rule takes only applications with X=1. In this case, no information on $P(D'|X=0)$ will be generated, though additional information on $P(D'|X=1)$ will be. This illustrates the difference between the two central questions: First, are loans being made that shouldn't be made (a question that can be answered using estimates of $P(D'|X=1)$)? Second, are loans that should be made not being made (a question that must be answered using $P(D'|X=0)$, on which there is no data)?

Note that $P(Y|X)$ can be estimated, and such an estimate might help an outside examiner trying to determine, for example, whether an institutional loan policy satisfies various legal requirements. Nevertheless, it does not provide information on $P(D'|X)$.

IV. Hidden Variables and Selectivity

The potential for biases in using the accepted loan data only arises when the selection mechanism proxies for omitted, but important, variables in the default equation. To see this in our Markov setup, we augment the variables by including the hidden variable U. Thus

$$(X,U) \rightarrow (Y,X,U) \rightarrow (D,Y,X)$$

If U was observed, the problem duplicates the previous one; if not, things become more complicated. Specifically, we would like to estimate $P(D'|X)$, the conditional probability of default given characteristics, marginally with respect to the hidden U, on the basis of our observed data, which are $P(D'|X,Y)$. In the previous section, $P(D'|X)$ and $P(D'|X,Y)$ were the same, because Y carried no relevant information given X. In the present case, Y might be relevant as a proxy for U. This is the case referred to as not missing at random, NMAR.

This point can be made in the simpler context of inference on the marginal probability of default. Thus we focus temporarily on the selection issue and abstract that issue from the problem of inference on the effects of the X variables. The chain becomes

$$U \rightarrow (Y,U) \rightarrow (D,Y)$$

and we wish to make inference on $P(D')$ on the basis of the data, which are informative on $P(D'|Y=1)$. Now, $P(D')$ is the marginal probability of default in the population, given by

$$P(D') = \int P(D'|U)g(U)dU,$$

while

$$P(D'|Y=1) = \int P(D'|U,Y)g(U|Y)dU$$
$$= \int P(D'|U)g(U|Y)dU$$

(the second equality holds since Y carries no new information given U). Here g(U) is the marginal distribution of U in the population and g(U|Y) is the conditional distribution. Thus

$$P(D'|Y=1) \neq P(D')$$

unless Y and U are independent. Hence using information on the accepted loans to make inference about the population default probability leads to bias.

The argument is easily extended to inference about the effects of characteristics X on the conditional distribution $P(D'|X)$ using data generated by the distribution $P(D'|X,Y=1)$. If the hidden variable U affects D' and Y, then Y will proxy for the effect of U in $P(D'|X,Y=1)$, leading to incorrect inferences. Note that

$$P(D'|X,U,Y=1) = P(D'|X,\underline{U}),$$

so Y is irrelevant given U and X. Nevertheless

$$P(D'|X,Y=1) \neq P(D'|X).$$

It is only through the interdependence of Y and the missing hidden variable U that bias arises.

V. Interpretation of U

What is the hidden variable U? This is not so clear. One obvious example arises when a variable used in scoring, and relevant for predicting default, does not enter the default probability model. It would be a clear mistake to include a variable in the scoring model that was not in the default model (although one could argue that not all variables in the default model need appear in the scoring model); thus, we suspect that this is not a likely source of bias.

8

The key is that the hidden variable must affect the decision to approve the loan and the default probability. This variable can be observed by whoever makes the lending decision but not by the default modeler. If loans are made in person, for example, an experienced loan officer may be able to get a "feel" that the applicant is more (or less) reliable than the paper data indicates. There may be many components to this "feel" not reflected in the application data: promptness in showing up for appointments, openness vs. shiftiness, vagueness or precision in answering questions. Such observations will affect the loan decision and, if they are accurate, also the default probability. If the variable is observed by the loan originator and used in the acceptance decision, but is in fact not relevant to the default probability, there will be no induced bias in using the default data on the accepted loans. Bias only arises if the data is relevant, is available to the acceptance decision maker and used, and is not available to the default modeler.

This bias cannot be corrected without adding information. One source of information is a priori – parametric assumptions on the joint distribution of Y and D given X, $P(Y,D|X)$. If these assumptions are sufficient to allow estimation of the parameters of the distribution given only the selected data, then the bias can be corrected. This approach has led to a huge literature in labor economics, beginning with Heckman (1976). Of course, a better source of information is more data. Impractical in the labor economics applications where the decisions are made by the same individual (the classical application has D' being wages or hours of work and Y employment), it is feasible when the institution determines Y and the applicant determines D'.

VI. Reject Inference

Modelers typically employ "reject sampling" or "reject inference" because they are concerned that potentially relevant information in the application data for rejected loans ought to be used in the default model. In this section we ask whether there is any relevant information in such data. *The answer is usually no.* That is, in studying default probabilities conditional on characteristics X, the relevant random variables generating

9

information about the probabilities of interest, are the default/nondefault records. The additional X variables alone are not of great interest in studying defaults (although they are of course informative on the scoring process, since the associated dependent variable accept/reject is observed).

Many reject sampling procedures assign values of the missing dependent variable, default/non-default, for the rejected applications according to the values of the X variables. This phase is referred to as "data augmentation." These values then enter a secondary analysis as real data. But the new default values are not random variables relevant to inference about defaults. That is, they are not default data. They are functions (possibly stochastic) of the existing default data. On a purely conceptual basis we have

(X, D') for accepted loans

X' for rejected loans

(X,X',D',D'') = "augmented" data

We have not been specific about how the D'', the default history for the rejected loans, is constructed, but the details are irrelevant for the concept. Namely, the augmented data do not contain any information not in the original data X, D' and X'.

In this example, when the information content of the augmented data and the original data is the same, a proper data analysis (taking account of the singular conditional distribution of D' and D'' in the augmented data set) will get the same answers from either of the two data sets. If the augmented data set is analyzed as though it were real data, the results will reflect the assignment D''. At the very least, the results will offer false precision, as illustrated below. If the assignment is arbitrary, the results may distort the information in the actual data.

Consider the simple example with X a single binary variable, and only one realized value chosen for the loan. There is information about only one of the default probabilities, corresponding to the chosen value of the X, not about both. The fact that one of the probabilities is unidentified is telling. If reject sampling produces a data set that purports to identify the other probability, it is being identified with non-data information. Thus suppose

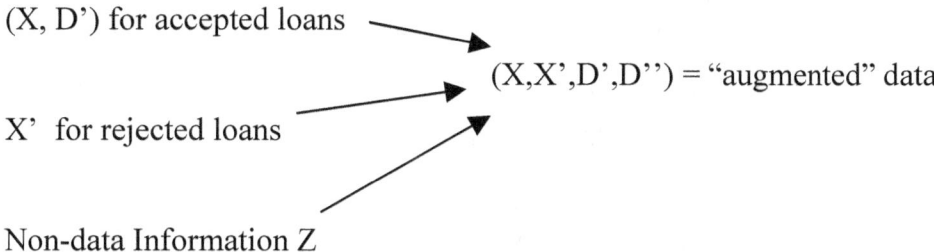

The non-data information Z consists of (in a common case) functional form assumptions or other assumptions made by the rejection sample design. For example, in our simple case the default probability for the value of X never accepted might just be assigned as, say, β. The result would be that an analysis of the augmented data set, treating it as a real data set, would discover that the default probability for the unselected value of X is β. But would it be sensible for a bank to base decisions on this kind of inference? The point is that the information being recovered by an analysis of the augmented data is generated by X, X', D' <u>and</u> Z. One should ask whether Z really deserves equal weight with the data?

Here is a less obvious, and less arbitrary, example. Suppose, in the context of our example with binary X, the acceptance decision is randomized so that there are some loans with X = 1 and some with X = 0. Then there is data information on both default probabilities. Suppose these are estimated from the accepted data as β_0 and β_1, corresponding to X=0 and X=1. We propose to assign default data (the dependent variable) to the X', the sample of application data from rejected loan applications. One way to do this would simply be to assign β_i as the value of the 0/1 variable D'' corresponding to X'=i. These non 0/1 dependent variables will pose problems for some estimation methods, however. Another assignment method is simply to draw $D_i^{*'} = 1$ with probability β_i and zero otherwise. Another method in use is to assign, for each X*,

β_i observations to the sample of defaults and 1-β_i to the sample of non-defaults. Some methods multiply these fractions by a factor generating integer numbers of additional observations. The point is that no new information is contained in the augmented data set, though an analysis of the augmented data as though it were real data seems to produce much more precise parameter estimates than the accepted data alone. Here the non-data "information" Z is the assumption that defaults in the rejected sample look exactly like their predicted values on the basis of the accepted sample. Thus, bias is not introduced, but a false sense of precision is introduced.

Another common method of assignment is based on functional form assumptions. For example, suppose X is a continuous scalar variable and the dependence of the default probability on X is estimated by a logit model using data from the sample of loans extended. Suppose only values of X greater than a cutoff x* are selected. Then, the accepted sample has X > x* and the declined X <=x*. Under the assumption that the logit model holds throughout the range of X in the population, predicted default probabilities or predicted defaults can be made for the declined sample on the basis of information in the accepted sample. Adding these "observations" to the augmented data set will give seemingly more precise estimates of the same parameters used to generate the new observations. This is merely a classic example of double-counting.

Consider this effect in the case where the X are all the same, so the default probability to be estimated is simply the marginal default probability. Using the sample of n_1 accepted loans, we estimate this probability by $p^\wedge$ = #defaults/(#defaults+#non-defaults) with sampling variance $p^\wedge(1-p^\wedge)/n_1$. Now consider augmenting the dataset with information from the n_2 declined loan applications. Assign defaults to these applications using one of the methods described above (for example, for each new observation, assign $p^\wedge$ new defaults and 1-$p^\wedge$ new non-defaults). Using the augmented sample, we calculate a new estimate, $p^{\wedge\wedge}$ = # defaults in the augmented data/(n_1+n_2). Clearly $p^{\wedge\wedge} = p^\wedge$, so our procedure has not introduced bias. (Assuming that the acceptance mechanism is not informative about the default probability, $p^\wedge$ is a correct estimator for the default probability). However, the standard calculation of the sampling variance of the estimator gives $V(p^{\wedge\wedge}) = p^{\wedge\wedge}(1-p^{\wedge\wedge})/(n_1+n_2) = n_1/(n_1+n_2)$ times $V(p^{\wedge})$. If the accepted and declined samples are equal in size, the augmented data gives an estimator with one-half the variance as the accepted sample. The ridiculousness of this procedure is easily illustrated by a further extension. Suppose there are an additional n_3 people who did not apply. In this example, knowing the X for these people (everyone has the same X), we apply the same procedure. This leads to the new estimate $p^{\wedge\wedge\wedge} = p^{\wedge\wedge} = p^{\wedge}$, but now with estimated variance $p^{\wedge\wedge\wedge}(1-p^{\wedge\wedge\wedge})/(n_1+n_2+n_3)$. The opportunities for increased apparent precision here are endless . . .

VII. Reject Inference: Mixture Models

Mixture models allow use of the X data from rejected applications through modeling assumptions on the joint distribution of the X characteristics and defaults. That is, the rejected applications are certainly informative on the distribution of X. If an assumption on the relationship between the marginal distribution of X and the conditional distribution of D given X can be plausibly maintained, then the distribution of X can be informative on defaults in the rejected sample. Note that this is a very strong assumption.

To see how this works, suppose the population consists of two groups; "defaulters" and "non-defaulters," with population (unconditional) proportions π and $(1-\pi)$. The characteristics X data are generated in the population according to the mixture model $p(x) = \pi p_d(x) + (1-\pi)p_n(x)$, where p_d and p_n are the marginal distributions of characteristics in the default and non-default populations respectively.

The likelihood contribution of the ith observation from the accepted sample is the joint probability of default and X for those who default, namely $\pi p_d(x_i)$, and the joint probability of non-default and X for those who do not, $(1-\pi)p_n(x_i)$. The contribution of the jth observation from the reject sample is the marginal probability of X, namely

$$p(x_j) = \pi p_d(x_j) + (1-\pi)p_n(x_j),$$

and the likelihood function is the product of the likelihood contributions from both samples. A parametric model can be selected for each of the p_i distributions and these parameters can be estimated along with π. The object of primary interest is the conditional probability of default given x, and this is given by

$$P(D|X) = \pi p_d(X)/(\pi p_d(X) + (1-\pi)p_n(X)).$$

Feelders (2000) gives an example in which p_n and p_d are two different normal distributions. In this example he finds that the mixture approach (known to be the correct model) improves on an approach based on fitting a logistic regression using the complete data. Hand and Henley (1997) give an assessment similar to ours; without new information, perhaps in the form of functional form assumptions, reject inference is unlikely to be productive.

To illustrate just how dependent this approach is on functional form assumptions, note that the model can be estimated, and predicted default probabilities calculated, without any data whatever on defaults! Closely related techniques go by the names cluster analysis and discriminant analysis.

How can the data on rejected applicants plausibly be used? The only hope is to get measurements on some proxy for the dependent variable on default experience. Here, external data such as credit bureau data may be useful. If the bureau data are available, and the declined applicant shows an additional credit line, then the payment performance on that credit line could be used as a measure of the performance of the loan had it been extended. Of course, there are a number of assumptions that must be made here. These are practical matters (Was the loan extended similar to the loan that was declined, and do the loan terms affect the default behavior? Is the bureau information comparable to the data on existing loans?), but the possibility remains that data could be assembled on rejected applicants. The requirement here is that payment performance be measured, albeit with noise. It cannot simply be imputed.

VIII. Parametric Models

The X data used in default models typically contains continuous variables, for example, financial ratios, as well as discrete variables. It is natural to experiment with parameterized models, for the parsimonious description of the effects of these variables. A common specification is the logit, in which the log-odds follow the linear model $\ln(P(D'=1|x)/P(D'=0|x)) = x'\beta$, where x is a vector consisting of values of the elements of X and β is a vector of coefficients. This model can be fit to data on accepted loans. In the absence of bias due to relevant hidden variables and subject to well-known regularity conditions, the parameter β will be consistently estimated. Under the maintained assumption that the functional form of the relationship between the characteristics X and the default probability is the same in the accepted and declined samples, predicted values of the default probabilities in the declined sample are appropriate estimates of the default probabilities for those observations, and are appropriate for use as a scoring rule (or part of a scoring rule).

If the selection has been completely at random (MCAR), so the X configuration in the declined sample is the same as the X configuration in the accepted sample, we are on firm ground. However, if selection is on the basis of a particular element of x being greater than x*, say, then it is a matter of assumption that the effect of x values less than x* satisfy the same relation to default probabilities as x values greater than x*. This issue is similar to our example of the binary X used for selection. The default probability can be estimated only for the value of X selected. Assigning a default probability for the other value of X is a matter of assumption. Here, we are a little better off, though still relying on assumptions.

Economic relations being what they are, it is probably safe to assume that the effects of x less than x*, but near x*, have the same effect (in functional form) as those greater than x*, particularly if the specification has been rigorously checked within the sample and found to hold for all x greater than x*. Extending the prediction of default probabilities for values of x well outside the range of experience is dangerous. However, the loss here is small; the crucial thing is probably to sharpen prediction around the cutoff. It doesn't really matter whether a default probability is 0.6 or 0.7 if loans will be approved only if the probability is less than 0.05.

IX. Advantages of Parametric Modeling

Using a parametric model can lead to substantially more accurate measurement and predictions if the model is adequate. It is useful to illustrate with a brief example. Let the vector x take values in $\{x_1, x_2, \ldots, x_K\} = X$. Here each x_j is a 1 x q row vector with first element equal to 1 (so the model allows a constant mean probability as a special case – this is good statistical practice) and q-1 additional elements with values of individual characteristics. Consider the logistic regression model with default probability F^i for the ith observation (with characteristics x^i equal to one of the x_j)

$$F^i = F(x^i\beta) = 1/(1+\exp(-x^i\beta))$$

$$1-F^i = 1/(1+\exp(x^i\beta))$$

The parameter β is a q x 1 vector. The likelihood function is $L(\beta) = \prod_i (F^i)^{d_i}(1-F^i)^{1-d_i}$ where $d_i = 1$ if the ith observation defaulted and zero otherwise. The log-likelihood is

$$l(\beta) = \sum_i d_i \ln F_i + \sum_i (1 - d_i)\ln(1 - F_i)$$

Now let D_k be the number of defaults at $x=x_k$, and F_k the associated probability $F(x_k\beta)$ and N_k the number of observations i with $x^i = x_k$. Then

$$l(\beta) = \Sigma_k D_k \ln F_k + \Sigma_k(N_k-D_k)\ln(1-F_k)$$

with score function $s(\beta) = l_\beta(\beta)$

$$s(\beta) = \Sigma_k D_k x_k'(1-F_k) - \Sigma_k(N_k-D_k)x_k'F_k$$

using $\partial \ln F/\partial \beta = x'F(-x\beta) = x'(1-F)$. Then

$$s_\beta = -\Sigma_k N_k x_k' \partial F_k/\partial\beta$$

Use $\partial F_k/\partial\beta = x_{k'}(1-F_k)F_k$ to get

$$s_\beta = l_{\beta\beta} = \partial^2 l(\beta)/\partial\beta\partial\beta' = -\Sigma_k N_k x_k' x_k(1-F_k)F_k.$$

Note that the negative inverse of this non-stochastic matrix is the approximate variance of the MLE, $\beta^\wedge$.

Let the x_k be ordered so that F_K is the highest acceptable default probability (i.e., nearest the desired cutoff value for the scoring rule). F_K can be non-parametrically estimated by $F_K^\wedge = D_K/N_K$ with approximate variance $F_K^\wedge(1- F_K^\wedge)/N_K$. Specifically, $N_K^{1/2}(F_K^\wedge-F_K) \to N(0,F_K(1-F_K))$. Consider the alternative estimator $F_K^* = F(x_K\beta^\wedge)$, where $\beta^\wedge$ is the MLE. Here, under the additional assumption that N_k/N remains fixed, $N^{1/2}(F_K^* - F_K) \to N(0,V)$, where

$$V = \partial F_K/\partial\beta(-l_{\beta\beta}/N)^{-1}\partial F_K/\partial\beta'.$$

Recall that $\partial F_K/\partial\beta = x_K'(1-F_K)F_K$ and hence

$$V = x_K(-\Sigma_k N_k x_k' x_k(1-F_k)F_k)^{-1}x_K'(1-F_K)^2 F_K^2$$

The relevant variance comparison is between V/N and $(1-F_K)F_K/N_k$.

As an example we take $X = \{(1,1),(1,2),\ldots,(1,20)\} = \{x_1,\ldots,x_{20}\}$ and $F_k = 1/(1+\exp(-x_k \beta))$. To focus attention on the essential parameter, the second element of β, we break out the intercept and redefine β and x as scalars, writing $x_k\beta = \alpha + \beta x_k$ with $\alpha=-6.5$ and $\beta = 0.3$. We consider the accepted sample with $x < 12$. The cutoff probability is 0.04 and we are interested for the moment in estimating F_{11} (the true value at these parameters is 0.0392). With 1000 observations for each value of x, the standard error of the nonparametric estimator is 0.00613. The standard error $(V/N)^{1/2}$ is 0.00441. The precision of the estimated probability at $X = 11$ is clearly improved by using the information from other values of x and the functional form information. For the nonparametric estimator to achieve the same standard deviation would require a sample size at $X = 11$ of 1,932, nearly double the actual. For comparison, if the data at $X=12$ were also available, with 1,000 additional observations, the forecast standard error of F_{11} is reduced to 0.00316. If instead these additional 1,000 observations were spread evenly between 1 and 11 (values of X) the standard error would be 0.0042. Thus, values at 12 (near but beyond the cutoff) are more informative than additional values in the current sample range.

Parametric models also provide, by means of assumptions, a mechanism for out-of-sample predictions. For example, it is of considerable interest in our example to estimate F_{12}. Should these loans be made? We can use the in sample data non-parametrically to estimate F_{11} (perhaps these loans should not be made) but not F_{12}. On the other hand, the parametric model can be simply extrapolated to provide an estimate of F_{12}, though there is no data available to test the accuracy of the fit at $X = 12$. Thus nonparametric analysis of loans made can be informative on which loans that were made should not have been made. However, it cannot say anything about which loans not made should have been made. This is a clear argument for (cautious) parametric modeling.

X. Dangers of Parametric Modeling

Choosing the functional form is a difficult but standard statistical problem. The usual tradeoff between over-fitting and parsimony arises. A model that describes the sample exactly is nearly useless for prediction, as we expect there is noise in the default mechanism and a description of noise does not extend outside the sample. On the other hand, too much concern for parsimony will lead to forecasting the default probability by its mean. Not necessarily bad, but clearly improvable.

A simple example can illustrate the effects of misspecification. Suppose the above logit model, with simple linear log-odds, has been obtained by a modeler after analyzing data on loans extended under his bank's historical decision rule (i.e., extend loans for which X values < 12).

However, suppose that the process generating default probabilities has a quadratic effect of x. That is, suppose that, the "true" process is

$$\Pr(D=1|X=x) = (1+\exp\{-\alpha-\beta x-\gamma x^2\})^{-1}$$

where $\alpha = 10$, $\beta = 0.87$ and $\gamma = -0.025$.

As we illustate below, it is reasonable to think that the quadratic term's influence on performance would go undetected by the scoring model developer when only performance data on extended loans with X<12 have been used in development. While the estimators for α and β from the misspecified model will be inconsistent, the main questions of interest relate to the predicted probabilities and the amount of error therein.

To investigate this, we examine a misspecified model fit to data on X = 1,2,…,11, the values acceptable according to the current hypothesized scoring rule, and then predict F_{11} (which can be consistently predicted) and F_{12} (which cannot). Here first report limiting, asymptotic results: we solve the likelihood equations for the misspecified model by setting their expectation (under the true model) equal to zero by choice of parameters of the misspecified model. For $\alpha = 10$, $\beta = 0.87$ and $\gamma = -0.025$ we have $\hat{F}_{11}$ = 0.033 and $\hat{F}_{12}$ = 0.052. The true values are $F_{11} = 0.0306$ and $F_{12} = 0.0407$. The range of actual and predicted default probabilities is shown in Figure 1.

Figure 1: Performance of a Misspecified Logistic Model: Asymptotic Calculations (Misspecified Model Developed with X<12)

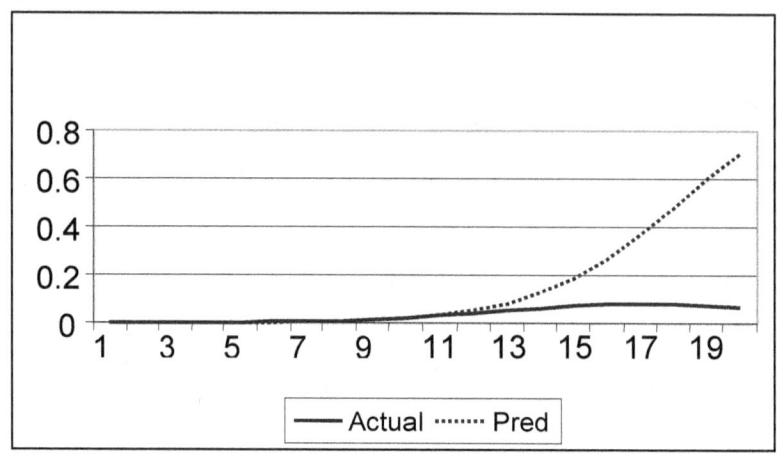

Figure 2 offers a closer look at the predicted and actual default probabilities for X < 15, and shows that the in-sample fit is quite good over most of the range:

Figure 2: Performance of a Misspecified Logistic Model: Asymptotic Calculations, A Close-Up View (Misspecified Model Developed with X<12)

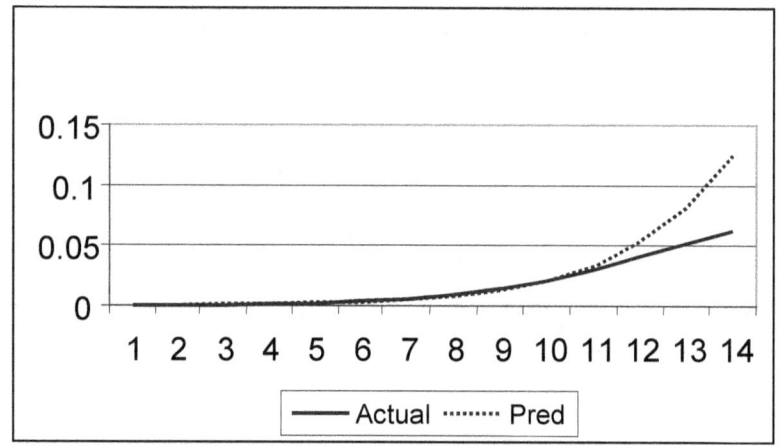

The parameter values in the examples were chosen so that most of the nonlinear effect shows up out of the available sample (X < 12). At these probability levels, these are probably values that a bank interested in expanding its loan portfolio, and willing to take on additional risk to do so, would be interested in forecasting accurately. That is, the bank currently cutting off at 11 might be interested in adding loans to applicants with X=12 or X=13. If the bank extends 100M$ in loans to a pool with X=12, it expects loss based on analysis of the existing sample of $F_{12}^{\wedge}*100M\$ = 5.2M\$$, but the actual expected loss is $F_{12}*100M\$ = 4.07M\$$. Clearly, there is substantial gain from accurate information about the out-of-sample losses.

In our example, in-sample parametric specification diagnostics will spot this misspecification if the sample is large. Thus, an asymptotic study along the above lines is feasible – the test is consistent. The question is, how large is large?

To investigate this question we use Monte Carlo techniques to run a small sampling experiment. We generate data from the quadratic logistic model above, fit a linear logistic model, and calculate predicted probabilities. We also calculate the likelihood ratio test for the linear vs. quadratic model (asymptotically equivalent to the score test but probably preferable in smaller samples). In fact, we see that the asymptotic results presented above can be misleading. The simple linear model is most often not rejected against the quadratic alternative within the $X < 12$ sample. Furthermore, the within-sample fit is much better than the asymptotic result, and the out-of-sample predictions are much worse. We use a model with a single, integer X, with values lower than 12 accepted into the loan sample and used in estimation. Of interest are the estimates of F_{11}, to verify whether this as a good cutoff point, and F_{12}, to ask whether additional loans could be made without substantially increasing risk.

First, we consider the likelihood ratio tests for the linear vs. quadratic models. We take 1,000 observations at each value of x, so each model is estimated with 11,000 observations. This is certainly a small sample relative to those seen in practice, but keep in mind we are using only one regressor (typical models in use would use many more). It is our intent to illustrate the general possibilities for poor sampling behavior rather than to analyze a particular model in current use. We estimate the model 200 times and calculate the predicted probabilities in-sample and out-of-sample as well as the likelihood ratio test for the significance of the quadratic term. The mean "p-value" is 0.296. If we test at the 0.10, 0.05 and 0.01 nominal significance levels we reject the linear model 33.5 percent, 23.5 percent, and 9.0 percent of the time respectively. Thus, the wrong model would probably not be rejected in practice. The predicted (mean) and actual probabilities are shown in Figure 3.

Figure 3: Performance of a Misspecified Logistic Model: Monte Carlo Calculations (Misspecified Model Developed with X<12)

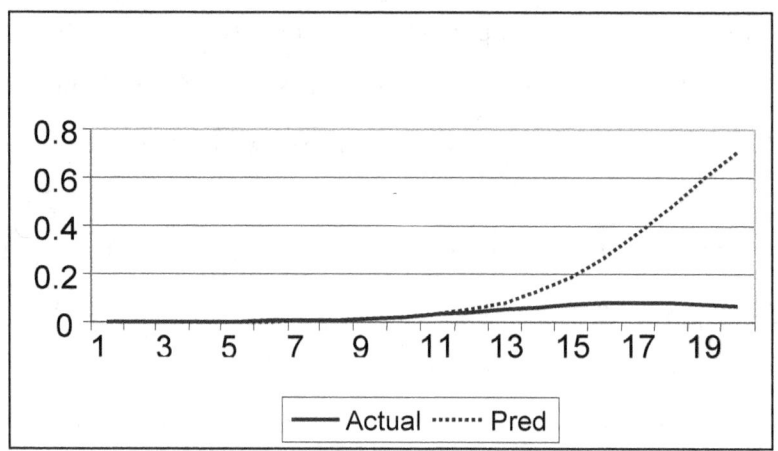

A closer look at the lower values of x shows that the within-sample fit is in fact quite good, although we have seen that the misspecification will be detected asymptotically.

Figure 4: A Close-Up View: Performance of a Misspecified Logistic Model: Monte Carlo Calculations (Misspecified Model Developed with X<12)

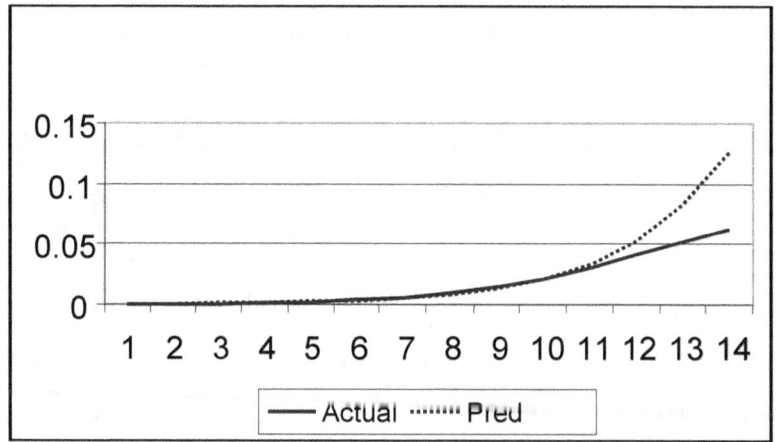

The asymptotic results on misspecification well characterize the sampling behavior of the estimators in the misspecified model. Here the estimates of F_{11} and F_{12} (recall the true values are 0.0306 and 0.0407) are 0.033 and 0.052. Thus the barely out-of-sample loss is overestimated, perhaps discouraging the bank from making good loans. The nonparametric estimators are $F_{11}^{NP} = 0.030$ and $F_{12}^{NP} = 0.041$. The former is feasible under our assumptions, the latter is not, since no loans are extended for $X = 12$, but we include this calculation to show the utility of additional, nonparametric information.

Box plots showing the distribution of the errors in the predicted probabilities are shown in Figure 5.

Figure 5: Forecast Errors of a Misspecified Logistic Model: Monte Carlo Calculations (Misspecified Model Developed with X<12)

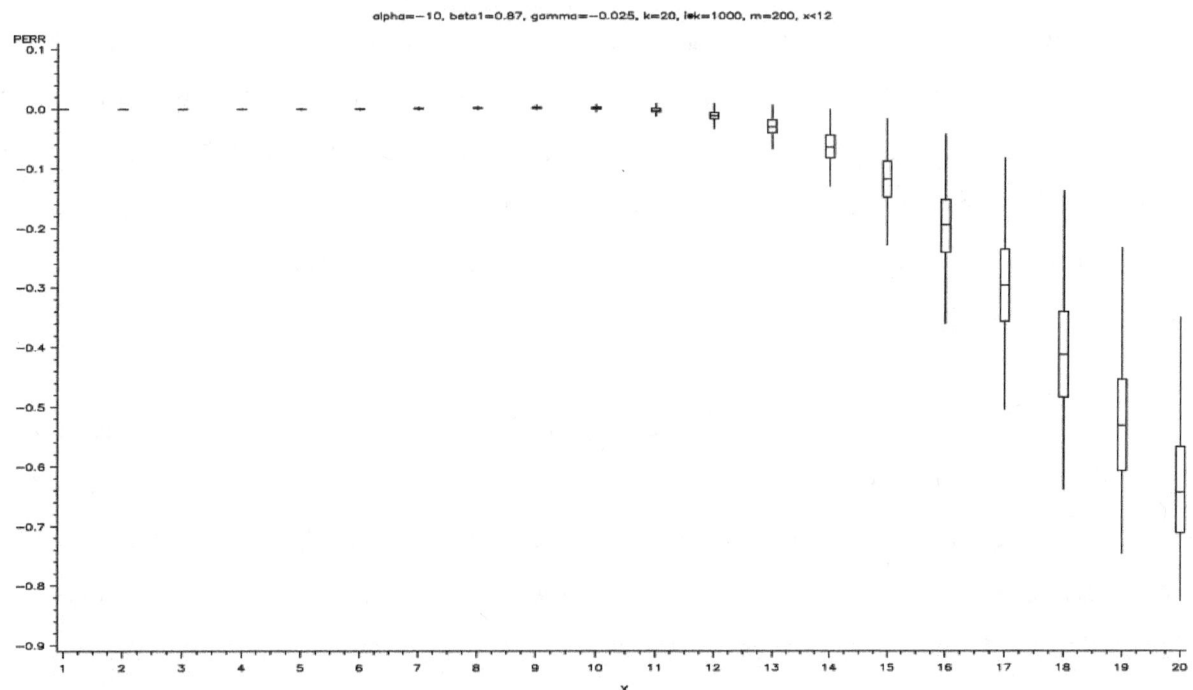

Note that, as expected, the prediction error is worse in terms of location and has higher variance as we predict farther out of the sample.

In fact, there are a wide variety of model selection mechanisms. A talented modeler, who will examine the fits of various models, logit and others, with different transformations of the variables, is invaluable. Automatic methods such as neural nets (a form of nonlinear regression) and other methods with automatic variable selection rules can also lead to good models for in-sample fits. Before developing models that forecast loan performance, modelers should consult lenders who will help them understand the financial and behavioral mechanisms involved.

XI. Experimentation

The bank is interested in precisely estimating default probabilities that are near the cutoff in the selection rule. Lending at this margin can give a bank its competitive edge. There are two issues: First, is the minimum acceptable default probability (in our example, the one for applicants at $F_{11)}$ well measured, and should loans continue to be made to these applicants? Second, should loans should be extended to the applicants considered marginally unacceptable — in our example, the applicants at F_{12}, and is $F_{12's}$ probability well forecast?

Note that the probabilities for F_{11} and F_{12} are estimated differently. There is direct data information on F_{11}; it can be estimated nonparametrically as well as parametrically, and specification errors can be detected, though this can be difficult in practice, as we have seen. There is no direct data information on F_{12}. It is not nonparametrically identified and can only be estimated with parametric assumptions.

Given the importance of correct measurement of these probabilities, the bank can be expected to devote considerable resources to getting these right. One way to devote resources to this effort is to make some loans at $X=12$. Suppose the same number of loan dollars are spread out from $X=1$ through 12, instead of from $X=1$ through 11. This will probably result in a riskier portfolio, since it is suspected that loans at X=12 are riskier than at X < 12. On the other hand, it is unlikely that loans at X=12 are much riskier than at X=11. Of course, the potential gain is that the improvement in measurement of F_{12} will reveal that these loans are indeed acceptable to the bank and should be made.

Note that the area of interest is the one around the cutoff value. Large changes in the selection rule are unlikely to be prudent. A good strategy would be to collect information, make small changes, re-estimate, etc. This suggests that loans at X=12 should not simply be substituted for those at X=11; the X=11 information is also critical to the measurement of risk at the cutoff. On the other hand, shifting portfolio dollars from X=11 to X=12 loans is cheaper than other shifts; why reject loans that are obviously profitable? We therefore consider this alternative strategy briefly after reporting our analysis of the initial experiment.

We consider the strategy of adding loans at X=12 by reducing the level of loans evenly across all other values of X. First, we do the asymptotic analysis. Here the sample size itself is irrelevant, though the even distribution of X across its possible values does affect the results. The most relevant probabilities are $F_{11}^P = 0.0299$ and $F_{12}^P = 0.0454$. Again, the true values are 0.0306 and 0.0407, so there is unambiguous improvement from adding this information at X = 12 (recall that the previous sample predicted $F_{12} = 0.052$). The predicted and actual probabilities over the whole range are shown in Figure 6.

Figure 6: Performance of a Misspecified Logistic Model: Asymptotic Calculations (Misspecified Model Developed with X<13)

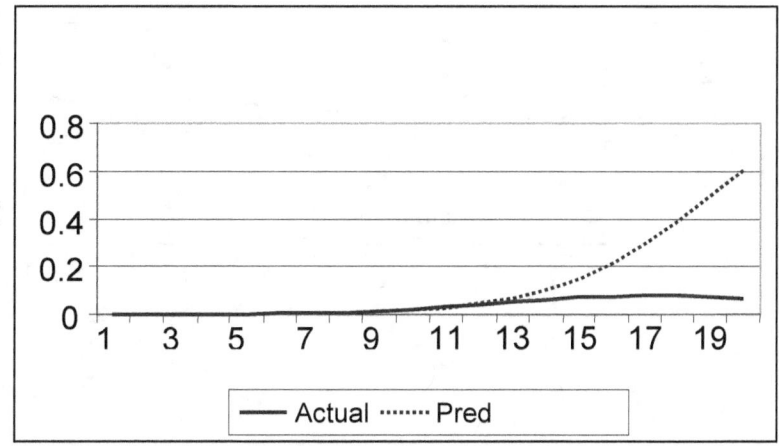

25

Next we turn to the sampling experiment. The total sample size for estimation remains the same, and we can directly compare the information value of observations at X=12 with that contained in the same number of observations distributed across all other levels of X. We now have 917 observations for each value of X = 1, 12. The resulting predicted probabilities F_{11}^P and F_{12}^P are 0.0301 and 0.0458 (recall the true values are 0.0306 and 0.0407) Thus, the additional information from the X = 12 observations substituted for some of the previous in-sample observations is indeed valuable, substantially improving the measurement of these probabilities. The nonparametric estimates are F_{11}^{NP} and F_{12}^{NP} = 0.031 and 0.041 respectively, now both feasible and clearly providing valuable information. The p-value for the LR test now has mean 0.20 and the linear model is rejected in favor of the quadratic at the 0.01, 0.05, and 0.10 nominal levels respectively 18.5 percent, 36 percent, and 49 percent of the time. Note that the additional information has both sharpened the estimates of F_{11} and F_{12} and improved the power of the specification test. The range of predicted and actual probabilities is show in Figure 7.

Figure 7: Performance of a Misspecified Logistic Model: Monte Carlo Calculations (Misspecified Model Developed with X<13)

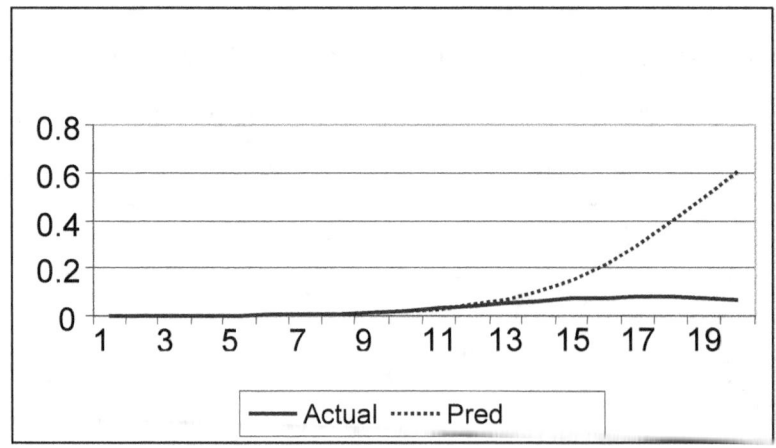

Figure 8 again looks more closely at the in-sample and barely out-of-sample predictions.

Figure 8: A Close-Up View: Performance of a Misspecified Logistic Model: Monte Carlo Calculations (Misspecified Model Developed with X<13)

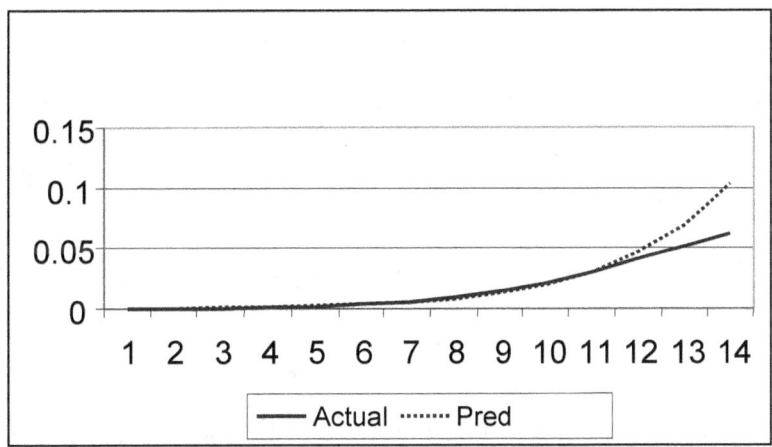

Once again the asymptotic results provide a good guide to the sampling performance of the estimators in the misspecified model. The box plot for the prediction errors is shown in Figure 9.

Figure 9: Forecast Errors of a Misspecified Logistic Model: Monte Carlo Calculations (Misspecified Model Developed with X<13)

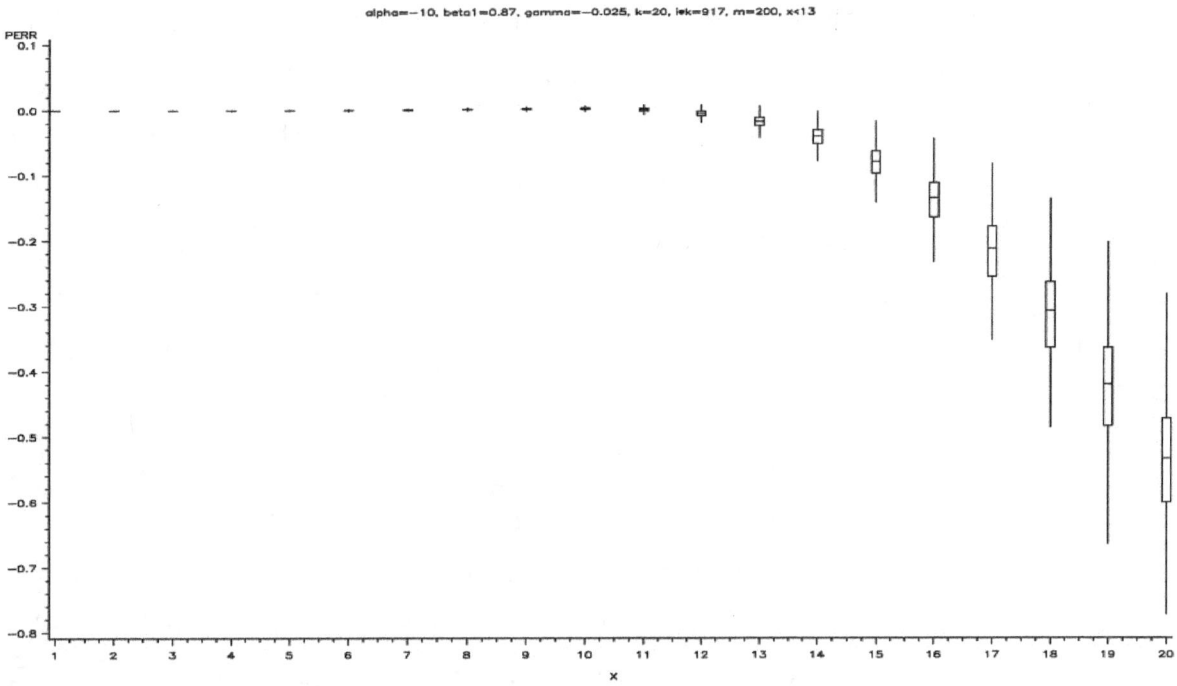

27

As we have seen before, the prediction errors are worse as we move away from the sampled values of characteristics X.

What is the cost of this experiment in terms of added loan portfolio risk? The average loan default probability with the cutoff at X <12 was estimated to be 0.0080 and the average probability with the cutoff at X<13 was estimated at 0.0117 before the additional data were accumulated. With the new estimates, the values are 0.0078 and 0.0110 respectively. The actual risk values are 0.0082 and 0.0109. The actual difference in risk is less than expected on the basis of either set of estimates, yet the addition is substantial.

An alternative experiment would continue to extend obviously good loans to the extent possible and to substitute loans at X=12 for those at X=11. The loans are substituted to keep the outstanding loan balance constant and hence make a fair comparison of the information value of the portfolio experience. Although X=11 loans are informative of behavior around the cutoff, and are therefore potentially important, the real key is the addition of the X=12 loans.

The asymptotic results give F_{11}^P and F_{12}^P as 0.0296 and 0.0449 (true 0.0306 and 0.0407) so there is clear improvement over the case in the X<12 sample and indeed even over the case of the X<13 sample with an even distribution. Thus, from this point of view, the addition of the new "extreme" value X=12 made the X=11 observations less relevant than the observations for lower values of X. Of course, this point cannot be pushed too far; with no observations at X=11 there is no nonparametric information on the default probability at that value.

Turning to the actual Monte Carlo results, we find that $F_{11}^P = 0.0296$ and $F_{12}^P = 0.0452$. These are quite good results as compared with the sample from X < 12 and indeed the sample with X<13 and spread observations. Because the graphs of predicted and actual probabilities are similar to those we have seen, they are omitted. Prediction errors get worse in terms of both location and variance as predictions occur farther away from sampled values. The likelihood ratio test shows improved performance. Rejections at the nominal 0.10, 0.05, and 0.01 levels are 53.5 percent, 40.0 percent, and 25.0 percent respectively. Thus the new, spread-out sample is informative about specification error.

Finally, we compare the risk of the portfolio with loans at X<12 with the portfolio of loans at X<13 and X -=11. The former we have calculated as 0.0082 (actual); the latter is 0.0091 (actual), a reduction from 0.011 at the spread-out sample. The less risky experiment is at least as informative as the riskier and is therefore clearly preferable.

While it is always speculative to generalize from examples, this analysis suggests that moving loans made near the current margin in the scoring cutoff just across the margin to accumulate information may be a sensible strategy. The information gain is considerable. The new information is particularly relevant to picking up misspecification that could go unnoticed within the current data range but which is important for assessing the performance of a scoring rule.

XII. Conclusions

This paper has emphasized key conceptual issues in the context of a stylized model of estimation and decision making. The distinction between parametric and nonparametric identification is illustrated with examples. We emphasize that there are two asymmetric questions one may ask of the data. First, should some of the loans with performance measures near the critical values not have been made? That is, should the critical value be adjusted so that some of the loans currently being approved will not be approved in the future? This question can be answered with data on current loans. Second, should some declined loan applications with estimated performance measures near the critical value have been approved? This question is much more difficult to answer, because one must use parametric assumptions if data comes solely from current loans. We illustrate some of the difficulties involved here, and emphasize the importance of in-sample specification checking. As a practical matter, additional data is invaluable. We illustrate some advantages of experimentation using loan applications with estimated performance measures near critical values. Modelers may be able to design experiments that, while not too costly in terms of portfolio performance, are extremely informative about the optimal loan decision procedure.

To conclude on a practical note, the actual process is not designed de novo, but is one in which procedures are changed (possibly even improved) by collecting additional data. Modeling this activity as a dynamic process, in which models are updated sequentially and experiments can be designed sequentially according to the likely value of the additional data, is the subject of a follow-up paper.

References:

H. Bierman and W. H. Hausman (1970), "The Credit Granting Decision," *Management Sci.,* 16, 519–532.

Boyes, W. J., D. L. Hoffman and S. A. Low (1989), "An Econometric Analysis of the Bank Credit Scoring Problem," *J. Ecmet*. 40: 3–14.

Carroll, R. J. and S. Pederson (1993), "On Robustness in the Logistic Regression Model," *JASA* 55:693–706.

Dirickyx, Y. M. I. and L. Wakeman (1976), "An Extension of the Bierman-Hausman Model for Credit Granting, *Management Sci.,* 22, 1229–1237.

Feelders, A. J.(2000), "Credit Scoring and Reject Inference with Mixture Models," *Int. J. Intell. Sys. Acc. Fin. Mgmt.* 9: 1-8.

D. J. Hand (1997), *Construction and Assessment of Classification Rules,* John Wiley. Chichester, U.K.

Hand, D. J. (2001), "Modelling Consumer Credit Risk," *IMA Journal of Management Mathematics* 12, 139-155.

Hand, D. J. and W. E. Henley (1997), "Statistical Classification Methods in Consumer Credit Scoring: A Review," *Journal of Roy. Statistical Soc. 5cr. A,* 160, 523–541.

Heckman, J. J. (1976), "The Common Structure of Statistical Models of Truncation, Sample Selection and Limited Dependent Vaiables, and a Simple Estimator for Such Models," *Annals of Economic and Social Measurement* 5: 475-492.

Little, Roderick J. A. and Donald B. Rubin (2002), *Statistical Analysis with Missing Data,* 2nd Edition, Hoboken. John Wiley & Sons.

Srinivasan, V. and Y. H. Kim (1987A), "The Bierman-Hausman Credit Granting Model:

A Note," *Management Sci.,* 33, 1361-1362.

Thomas, L.C., D. B. Edelman and J.N. Crook (2002), *Credit Scoring and Its Applications*, SIAM, Philadelphia.

Thomas, L.C., J.N. Crook and D. B. Edelman (1992), *Credit Scoring and Credit Control,* Oxford University Press, Oxford.